AF797647

ORGANIZE YOUR MOVE

A Packing and Relocation Workbook

www.wildrose-media.com

Organize Your Move: A Packing and Relocation Workbook

©2024 Wildrose Media. USA.
ISBN: 978-1-953489-33-3

All rights reserved. No part of this publication may be reproduced, distributed or transmitted in any form or by any means without prior written permission of the publisher except in the case of brief quotations for critical reviews and certain other noncommercial uses permitted by copyright law.

YOU MAY ALSO LIKE

HOME BUYER'S NOTEBOOK

New Home-Buying Checklists and more!

Available on Amazon ISBN: 978-1-953489-29-6

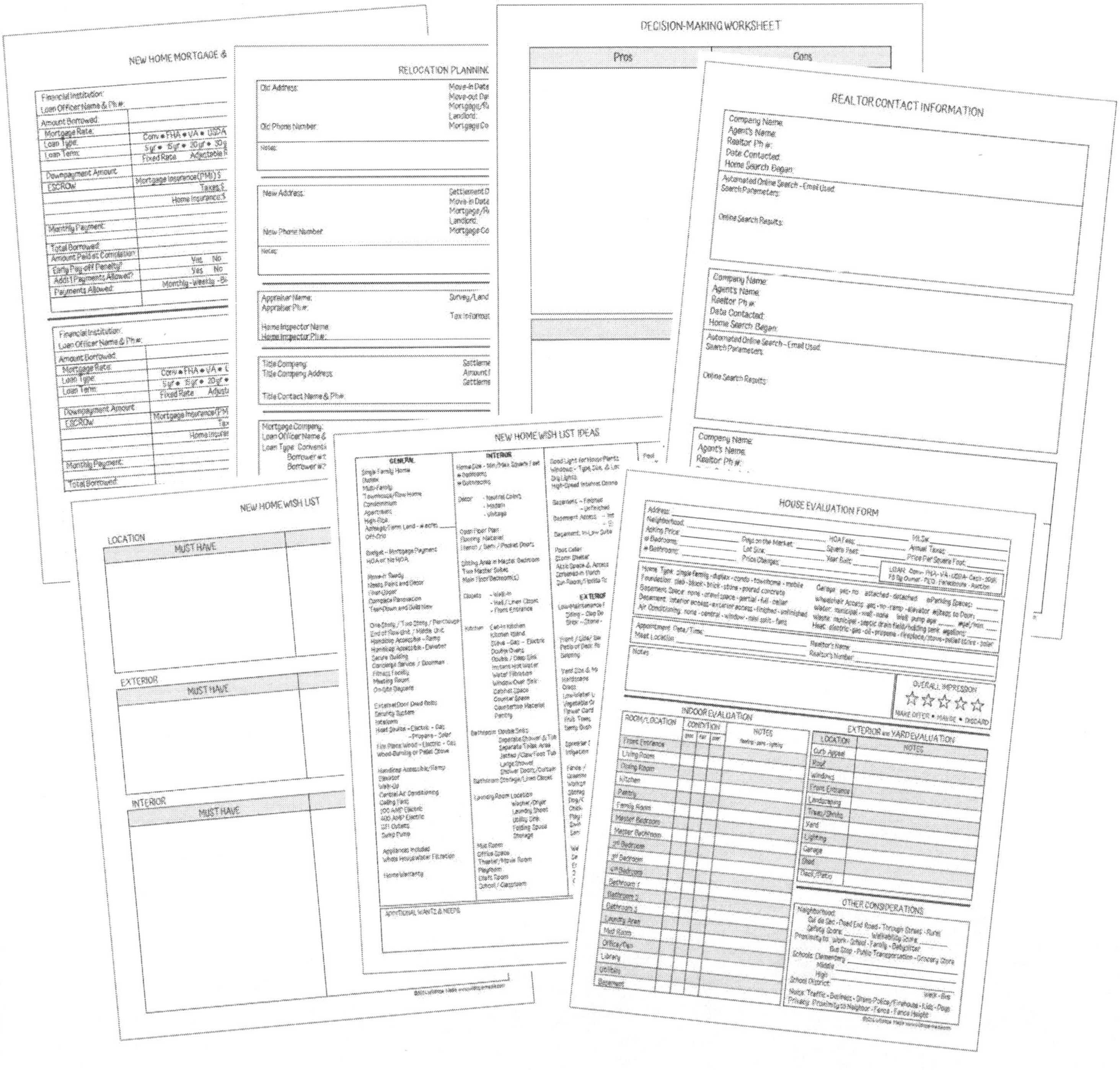

www.wildrose-media.com

TABLE OF CONTENTS

Introduction & How To Use This Notebook

I originally created this book for myself to help with our recent move. Since this relocation had been anticipated for months, I began packing weeks ahead of our move-date. Of course, packing so far in advance meant the possibility of needing items which had already been packed. To solve this problem I created a color-coded system to label the boxes and track their contents.

My system worked very well and our big move went smoothly, much more efficient and easier than in my previous experience.

In this notebook I'll share the worksheets and the process I used so that you, too can enjoy an efficient and stress-free move. (well, as stress free as moving can be!)

First, I assigned each room/area of our home a color using the "Box Inventory Overview- Room & Box Color Key" worksheet Once I had a unique color assigned to each location, I attached a sticker colored to match my color key onto several boxes. To make seeing it easier as it was carried or after it was stacked I used three stickers per box, placing one on the top and two on opposite sides of each box.

When I was ready to pack up an area, I moved the correctly color-coded box to the desired location and filled it. As I packed I used the "Detailed Box Inventory" pages to list the contents of each box. These lists are specific to each room (see the complete room list in the Table of Contents) though to ensure your home's specific needs are met, I included four blank inventory sheets as well.

Always price-conscious, I checked several moving/truck rental companies for estimates, so I included two worksheets for this as well. These are titled, "Moving Company Price Estimates Worksheet". With space for two companies on each page, you can get quotes from up to four movers/rental companies. When you've decided on a company, utilize the "Our Moving Company" worksheet to record more specific details including pick-up date and time, location, and additional supplies offered (such as dolly, packing blankets).

The "Moving Day Timeline" is included to help ensure no detail is missed or forgotten. This worksheet is divided into several blocks so you can write timed goals and anticipated events for moving day. The "Moving Day Helper" worksheet provides ample space to write your helpers contact info, expected arrival time, and compensation, as well as any box packers/un-packers and house-cleaners you may hire.

The "Box Arrival Checklist" worksheet and the "Furniture Arrival Checklist" are pretty self-explanatory. As these items/boxes arrive, check they are accounted for by marking them off the list.. Note- on moving day it helps to place a colored tag at the entrance (or over the doorway) to each room as well, so if you are not available the movers know where each box should be placed.

Other lists I used and included which you may also find helpful include:

House Cleaning Checklist
Utilities Reminders - to set up/transfer/remove utility services
Address Change Checklist - a reminder to notify others of your new contact info.

Some Packing Advice

- Protecting Fragile Items:

I ship items from home, so I used my padded shipping envelopes to wrap and protect fragile items.

When I was finished unpacking, they resumed their intended purpose.

- Canning Jars:

I make homemade jelly, so to protect the canning jars during the move I placed a sock over each one..
(I save the boxes the jars came in and they fit fine even with the socks on).

- If possible, load your storage and books shelves last. Then these will be the first off the moving truck and can be Immediately available to accept unloaded items which belong in that location.

Best wishes and safe travels as you relocate. And congratulations on your new home!

Wildrose Media

P.S. If you prefer a printable PDF version of this workbook, visit my website store @ www.wildrose-media.com

DECLUTTERING TIPS

The 5-Bin Method for Decluttering

The goal in decluttering is to get rid of anything you don't need, want, or like. Most organizers recommend using a 5 (or 6) bin method for sorting items during the declutter process. To do this obtain the following: 1 large trash bag, 1 box labeled *donate*, 1 box or plastic bin labeled *sell*, 1 box or bin labeled *keep*, 1 box or bin labeled *return*, and one box or bin labeled *repair*. If you like you can also add boxes labeled *sentimental* and *maybe/unsure*.

1. Trash

Contents of the trash bag are pretty obvious. Trash includes items which are broken, outdated, or spoiled.
Keep in mind certain items such as medications, glass, and hazardous waste must be disposed of safely and properly.

2. Keep

This box will contain any items which fit, are currently in use, are in good working condition, and that you have a place for. *Keep* items may include:

- small appliances which are used frequently
- seasonal decor
- seasonal clothing
- photos, personal mementos
- items which will be needed in the near future - such as maternity clothes or baby items

3. Sell

Items which you no longer need, want, or are duplicates can be sold as long as they are in good condition.
Social media marketplaces and neighborhood sites are great places to post and get a quick response.
Hosting a yard or garage sale is an additional but more time-intensive way to earn a few bucks.
Consignment stores offer a fast and easy way to rid yourself of unwanted items, though you will receive a pittance of what the item is worth. However, if you have the time and inclination, consignment sales are a good option. These are held seasonally, check the internet for upcoming local sales.

4. Donate

Items which you don't want to sell but are still in decent condition belong in this box.
Keep in mind, family, friends, and neighbors may be interested in your stuff- offer it to them first.
If not, some schools, churches, and libraries accept donations of toys, games, puzzles, books, clothing, and furniture. Many charity organizations offer free item pickup service and a tax-deductible receipt.
For more information on donations, visit my blog, Faith Family Fun on Wildrose-Media.com.
blog link: https://wildrose-media.com/donations-101-the-scoop-on-what-where-and-how-to-donate-your-unwanted-items/

5. Sentimental Items

These are items that are special to us, often because they are associated with a person or cherished memory.
Some ideas for parting with sentimental items include:

- take a photo or video of the item prior to removing from home
- for larger items, give the item to a family member who has use and space for it (bonus - you can visit it!)
- for smaller items, make a memento box to give to family members. Include a handwritten note about the items in each box and what makes them special.

6. Unsure/Don't know what to do with

If the idea of getting rid of stuff has you stressed out, try using this box. Set it aside and re-evaluate in 6 months.

TO DO LIST

MOVING SUPPLY CHECKLIST

- ❑ Moving Notebook
- ❑ Pen or Pencil with Eraser
- ❑ Bubble Wrap, Padded Envelopes, Foam Pouches
- ❑ Packing Paper, Tissue Pape, Rags, Old Clothes, Towels & Sheets – to wrap fragile items or to protect items from scratches
- ❑ Newspaper – to protect fragile items & to fill a partially full box (ink will transfer to items so wrap with plain paper first)
- ❑ Cardboard Boxes: Small – for fragile and heavier items like glassware, knickknacks & books

  Medium – kitchen items, toys, shoes & clothes

  Large – light or bulky items such as bedding, stuffed animals, lampshades
- ❑ Specialty Boxes – with dividers for glassware, large flat boxes for television, etc. (available at truck rental locations)
- ❑ Mattress Bags – to keep Mattresses clean and dry
- ❑ Heavy-Duty Packing Tape (with Tape Dispenser if preferred)
- ❑ Felt-Tipped Permanent Marker to Label Boxes
- ❑ Colored Labels or White Labels and Felt-Tipped Markers in Multiple Colors – to Color-code Boxes by Room
- ❑ Scissors
- ❑ Utility Knife (with extra blades) – to Open Boxes upon Arrival
- ❑ Tools for Disassembling and Reassembling Furniture:

  Screwdriver, Socket Set, Allen key, Wrench, Hammer

  Fully Charged Battery (if using Electric Tools)
- ❑ Plastic Baggies to secure loose screws and washers from disassembled furniture (be sure to label each bag!)
- ❑ Dolly for Heavy Items
- ❑ Furniture Slides – to place under legs
- ❑ Zip Ties – to secure cords
- ❑ Plastic Wrap – to secure drawers & protect furniture and other large items
- ❑ Packing Blankets (can be rented from moving company)
- ❑ Bungy Cords
- ❑ Ramp or Boards
- ❑ Door Stop or Rope to Hold Doors Open when Removing/Placing Items
- ❑ Trash Bags
- ❑ Hand Wipes and Hand Sanitizer
- ❑ Vacuum Cleaner
- ❑ Cleaning Solution, Wipes and/or Rags
- ❑ Fully Charged Cellphone

MOVING COMPANY PRICE ESTIMATES

Information Necessary for Estimates

Square Footage of Old Home: Date Needed:
Distance:
Number of Rooms: Stairs Old Home: Yes No Old Home #/Flights of Stairs:
Estimated # Boxes: Stairs New Home: Yes No Old Home #/Flights of Stairs:
Heavy or Specialty Items to Be Moved:
Freezer: Yes No Safe: Yes No Gun Cabinet Yes No

Estimates:

Moving Company Name:
Referred By:
Contact Name & Ph #:
Type of Truck/Truck Size:
Moving: Furniture Y N Special Instructions:
Moving Boxes Y N # Boxes:
Packing Service:
Unpacking Service:
Estimated # Hours:
Estimated Cost:
Amount of Deposit Required:
Additional Expenses:
Dolly/Hand Truck
Packing Blankets
Boxes & Packing Supplies
Helpers

Total Estimated Amount:

Moving Company Name:
Referred By:
Contact Name & Ph #:
Type of Truck/Truck Size:
Moving: Furniture Y N Special Instructions:
Moving Boxes Y N # Boxes:
Packing Service:
Unpacking Service:
Estimated # Hours:
Estimated Cost:
Amount of Deposit Required:
Additional Expenses:
Dolly/Hand Truck
Packing Blankets
Boxes & Packing Supplies
Helpers

Total Estimated Amount:

©2024 Wildrose Media www.wildrose-media.com

MOVING COMPANY PRICE ESTIMATES

Information Necessary for Estimates

Square Footage of Old Home: Date Needed:
Distance:
Number of Rooms: Stairs Old Home: Yes No Old Home #/Flights of Stairs:
Estimated # Boxes: Stairs New Home: Yes No Old Home #/Flights of Stairs:
Heavy or Specialty Items to Be Moved:
Freezer: Yes No Safe: Yes No Gun Cabinet Yes No

Estimates:

Moving Company Name:
Referred By:
Contact Name & Ph #:
Type of Truck/Truck Size:
Moving: Furniture Y N Special Instructions:
Moving Boxes Y N # Boxes:
Packing Service:
Unpacking Service:
Estimated # Hours:
Estimated Cost:
Amount of Deposit Required:
Additional Expenses:
- Dolly/Hand Truck
- Packing Blankets
- Boxes & Packing Supplies
- Helpers

Total Estimated Amount:

Moving Company Name:
Referred By:
Contact Name & Ph #:
Type of Truck/Truck Size:
Moving: Furniture Y N Special Instructions:
Moving Boxes Y N # Boxes:
Packing Service:
Unpacking Service:
Estimated # Hours:
Estimated Cost:
Amount of Deposit Required:
Additional Expenses:
- Dolly/Hand Truck
- Packing Blankets
- Boxes & Packing Supplies
- Helpers

Total Estimated Amount:

©2024 Wildrose Media www.wildrose-media.com

OUR MOVING COMPANY

Moving Company Name:
Referred By:
Contact Name & Ph #:
Truck Size:
Moving: Furniture Y N   Special Instructions:
Moving Boxes Y N   # Boxes

Estimated Cost:
Deposit Paid:
Additional Expenses:
- Gas
- Food
- Supplies
- Helpers
- Tip

Total Amount Paid:

Estimated # Hours: Actual # Hours:
Scheduled Arrival Time: Actual Arrival Time:
Start Time: Completion Time:

Names of Movers:

Packing/Unpacking Helpers:

Notes:

©2024 Wildrose Media www.wildrose-media.com

BOX INVENTORY OVERVIEW: ROOM & COLOR CODE KEY

Location	Color Code	# Boxes	Notes
Family Room	☐		
Living Room	☐		
Dining Room	☐		
Kitchen	☐		
Pantry	☐		
Mud Room	☐		
Laundry Room	☐		
Master Bedroom	☐		
Master Bathroom	☐		
Bathroom 1	☐		
Bathroom 2	☐		
Bathroom 3	☐		
Bedroom 1	☐		
Bedroom 2	☐		
Bedroom 3	☐		
Bedroom 4	☐		
Den	☐		
Office	☐		
Books	☐		
Playroom	☐		
Classroom/School	☐		
Theater Room	☐		
Craft Room	☐		
Storage Room	☐		
Attic	☐		
Basement	☐		
Workshop	☐		
Garage	☐		
Shed	☐		
Donate	☐		
	☐		

©2024 Wildrose Media www.wildrose-media.com

Box Inventory: Family Room

Family Room Box Label Color:

Family Room Box #_____

Family Room Box #_____

Family Room Box #_____

Family Room Box #_____

Family Room Box #_____

Family Room Box #_____

Family Room Box #_____

Family Room Box #_____

Box Inventory: Family Room

Family Room Box Label Color:

Family Room Box #_____

Family Room Box #_____

Family Room Box #_____

Family Room Box #_____

Family Room Box #_____

Family Room Box #_____

Family Room Box #_____

Family Room Box #_____

Box Inventory: Living Room

Living Room Box Label Color:

Living Room Box #_____

Living Room Box #_____

Living Room Box #_____

Living Room Box #_____

Living Room Box #_____

Living Room Box #_____

Living Room Box #_____

Living Room Box #_____

Box Inventory: Living Room

Living Room Box Label Color:

Living Room Box #_____

Living Room Box #_____

Living Room Box #_____

Living Room Box #_____

Living Room Box #_____

Living Room Box #_____

Living Room Box #_____

Living Room Box #_____

Box Inventory: Dining Room

Dining Room Box Label Color:

Dining Room Box #_____

Dining Room Box #_____

Dining Room Box #_____

Dining Room Box #_____

Dining Room Box #_____

Dining Room Box #_____

Dining Room Box #_____

Dining Room Box #_____

Box Inventory: Dining Room

Dining Room Box Label Color:

Dining Room Box #_____

Dining Room Box #_____

Dining Room Box #_____

Dining Room Box #_____

Dining Room Box #_____

Dining Room Box #_____

Dining Room Box #_____

Dining Room Box #_____

Box Inventory: Kitchen

Kitchen Box Label Color:

Kitchen Box #______

Kitchen Box #______

Kitchen Box #______

Kitchen Box #______

Kitchen Box #______

Kitchen Box #______

Kitchen Box #______

Kitchen Box #______

Box Inventory: Kitchen

Kitchen Box Label Color: ◯

Kitchen Box #_____

Kitchen Box #_____

Kitchen Box #_____

Kitchen Box #_____

Kitchen Box #_____

Kitchen Box #_____

Kitchen Box #_____

Kitchen Box #_____

Box Inventory: Pantry

Pantry Box Label Color:

Pantry Box #_____

Pantry Box #_____

Pantry Box #_____

Pantry Box #_____

Pantry Box #_____

Pantry Box #_____

Pantry Box #_____

Pantry Box #_____

Box Inventory: Pantry

Pantry Box Label Color:

Pantry Box #______

Pantry Box #______

Pantry Box #______

Pantry Box #______

Pantry Box #______

Pantry Box #______

Pantry Box #______

Pantry Box #______

Box Inventory: Mud Room

Mud Room Box Label Color:

Mud Room Box #_____

Mud Room Box #_____

Mud Room Box #_____

Mud Room Box #_____

Mud Room Box #_____

Mud Room Box #_____

Mud Room Box #_____

Mud Room Box #_____

Box Inventory: Mud Room

Mud Room Box Label Color:

Mud Room Box #_____

Mud Room Box #_____

Mud Room Box #_____

Mud Room Box #_____

Mud Room Box #_____

Mud Room Box #_____

Mud Room Box #_____

Mud Room Box #_____

Box Inventory: Laundry Room

Laundry Room Box Label Color:

Laundry Room Box #_____

Laundry Room Box #_____

Laundry Room Box #_____

Laundry Room Box #_____

Laundry Room Box #_____

Laundry Room Box #_____

Laundry Room Box #_____

Laundry Room Box #_____

Box Inventory: Laundry Room

Laundry Room Box Label Color:

Laundry Room Box #_____

Laundry Room Box #_____

Laundry Room Box #_____

Laundry Room Box #_____

Laundry Room Box #_____

Laundry Room Box #_____

Laundry Room Box #_____

Laundry Room Box #_____

Box Inventory: Master Bedroom

Master Bedroom Box Label Color:

Master Bedroom Box #______

Master Bedroom Box #______

Master Bedroom Box #______

Master Bedroom Box #______

Master Bedroom Box #______

Master Bedroom Box #______

Master Bedroom Box #______

Master Bedroom Box #______

Box Inventory: Master Bedroom

Master Bedroom Box Label Color:

Master Bedroom Box #_____

Master Bedroom Box #_____

Master Bedroom Box #_____

Master Bedroom Box #_____

Master Bedroom Box #_____

Master Bedroom Box #_____

Master Bedroom Box #_____

Master Bedroom Box #_____

Box Inventory: Master Bathroom

Master Bathroom Box Label Color:

Master Bathroom Box #_____

Master Bathroom Box #_____

Master Bathroom Box #_____

Master Bathroom Box #_____

Master Bathroom Box #_____

Master Bathroom Box #_____

Master Bathroom Box #_____

Master Bathroom Box #_____

Box Inventory: Master Bathroom

Master Bathroom Box Label Color: ◯

Master Bathroom Box #______

Master Bathroom Box #______

Master Bathroom Box #______

Master Bathroom Box #______

Master Bathroom Box #______

Master Bathroom Box #______

Master Bathroom Box #______

Master Bathroom Box #______

Box Inventory: Bathroom 1

Bathroom 1 Box Label Color:

Bathroom 1 Box #_____

Bathroom 1 Box #_____

Bathroom 1 Box #_____

Bathroom 1 Box #_____

Bathroom 1 Box #_____

Bathroom 1 Box #_____

Bathroom 1 Box #_____

Bathroom 1 Box #_____

Box Inventory: Bathroom 1

Bathroom 1 Box Label Color:

Bathroom 1 Box #_____

Bathroom 1 Box #_____

Bathroom 1 Box #_____

Bathroom 1 Box #_____

Bathroom 1 Box #_____

Bathroom 1 Box #_____

Bathroom 1 Box #_____

Bathroom 1 Box #_____

Box Inventory: Bathroom 2

Bathroom 2 Box Label Color:

Bathroom 2 Box #______

Bathroom 2 Box #______

Bathroom 2 Box #______

Bathroom 2 Box #______

Bathroom 2 Box #______

Bathroom 2 Box #______

Bathroom 2 Box #______

Bathroom 2 Box #______

Box Inventory: Bathroom 2

Bathroom 2 Box Label Color:

Bathroom 2 Box #______

Bathroom 2 Box #______

Bathroom 2 Box #______

Bathroom 2 Box #______

Bathroom 2 Box #______

Bathroom 2 Box #______

Bathroom 2 Box #______

Bathroom 2 Box #______

Box Inventory: Bathroom 3

Bathroom 3 Box Label Color:

Bathroom 3 Box #_____

Bathroom 3 Box #_____

Bathroom 3 Box #_____

Bathroom 3 Box #_____

Bathroom 3 Box #_____

Bathroom 3 Box #_____

Bathroom 3 Box #_____

Bathroom 3 Box #_____

Box Inventory: Bathroom 3

Bathroom 3 Box Label Color:

Bathroom 3 Box #_____

Bathroom 3 Box #_____

Bathroom 3 Box #_____

Bathroom 3 Box #_____

Bathroom 3 Box #_____

Bathroom 3 Box #_____

Bathroom 3 Box #_____

Bathroom 3 Box #_____

Box Inventory: Bedroom 1

Bedroom 1 Box Label Color:

Bedroom 1 Box #______

Bedroom 1 Box #______

Bedroom 1 Box #______

Bedroom 1 Box #______

Bedroom 1 Box #______

Bedroom 1 Box #______

Bedroom 1 Box #______

Bedroom 1 Box #______

Box Inventory: Bedroom 1

Bedroom 1 Box Label Color:

Bedroom 1 Box #_____

Bedroom 1 Box #_____

Bedroom 1 Box #_____

Bedroom 1 Box #_____

Bedroom 1 Box #_____

Bedroom 1 Box #_____

Bedroom 1 Box #_____

Bedroom 1 Box #_____

Box Inventory: Bedroom 2

Bedroom 2 Box Label Color:

Bedroom 2 Box #______

Bedroom 2 Box #______

Bedroom 2 Box #______

Bedroom 2 Box #______

Bedroom 2 Box #______

Bedroom 2 Box #______

Bedroom 2 Box #______

Bedroom 2 Box #______

Box Inventory: Bedroom 2

Bedroom 2 Box Label Color:

Bedroom 2 Box #______

Bedroom 2 Box #______

Bedroom 2 Box #______

Bedroom 2 Box #______

Bedroom 2 Box #______

Bedroom 2 Box #______

Bedroom 2 Box #______

Bedroom 2 Box #______

Box Inventory: Bedroom 3

Bedroom 3 Box Label Color:

Bedroom 3 Box #_____

Bedroom 3 Box #_____

Bedroom 3 Box #_____

Bedroom 3 Box #_____

Bedroom 3 Box #_____

Bedroom 3 Box #_____

Bedroom 3 Box #_____

Bedroom 3 Box #_____

Box Inventory: Bedroom 3

Bedroom 3 Box Label Color: ◯

Bedroom 3 Box #______

Bedroom 3 Box #______

Bedroom 3 Box #______

Bedroom 3 Box #______

Bedroom 3 Box #______

Bedroom 3 Box #______

Bedroom 3 Box #______

Bedroom 3 Box #______

Box Inventory: Bedroom 4

Bedroom 4 Box Label Color: ◯

Bedroom 4 Box #_____

Bedroom 4 Box #_____

Bedroom 4 Box #_____

Bedroom 4 Box #_____

Bedroom 4 Box #_____

Bedroom 4 Box #_____

Bedroom 4 Box #_____

Bedroom 4 Box #_____

Box Inventory: Bedroom 4

Bedroom 4 Box Label Color:

Bedroom 4 Box #_____

Bedroom 4 Box #_____

Bedroom 4 Box #_____

Bedroom 4 Box #_____

Bedroom 4 Box #_____

Bedroom 4 Box #_____

Bedroom 4 Box #_____

Bedroom 4 Box #_____

Box Inventory: Den

Den Box Label Color:

Den Box #_____

Den Box #_____

Den Box #_____

Den Box #_____

Den Box #_____

Den Box #_____

Den Box #_____

Den Box #_____

Box Inventory: Den

Den Box Label Color: ◯

Den Box #_____

Den Box #_____

Den Box #_____

Den Box #_____

Den Box #_____

Den Box #_____

Den Box #_____

Den Box #_____

Box Inventory: Office

Office Box Label Color:

Office Box #_____

Office Box #_____

Office Box #_____

Office Box #_____

Office Box #_____

Office Box #_____

Office Box #_____

Office Box #_____

Box Inventory: Office

Office Box Label Color:

Office Box #_____

Office Box #_____

Office Box #_____

Office Box #_____

Office Box #_____

Office Box #_____

Office Box #_____

Office Box #_____

Box Inventory: Books

Books Box Label Color:

Books Box #______

Books Box #______

Books Box #______

Books Box #______

Books Box #______

Books Box #______

Books Box #______

Books Box #______

Box Inventory: Books

Books Box Label Color:

Books Box #______

Books Box #______

Books Box #______

Books Box #______

Books Box #______

Books Box #______

Books Box #______

Books Box #______

Box Inventory: Playroom

Playroom Box Label Color:

Playroom Box #_____

Playroom Box #_____

Playroom Box #_____

Playroom Box #_____

Playroom Box #_____

Playroom Box #_____

Playroom Box #_____

Playroom Box #_____

Box Inventory: Playroom

Playroom Box Label Color:

Playroom Box #_____

Playroom Box #_____

Playroom Box #_____

Playroom Box #_____

Playroom Box #_____

Playroom Box #_____

Playroom Box #_____

Playroom Box #_____

Box Inventory: Classroom/School

Classroom/School Box Label Color:

Classroom/School Box #_____

Classroom/School Box #_____

Classroom/School Box #_____

Classroom/School Box #_____

Classroom/School Box #_____

Classroom/School Box #_____

Classroom/School Box #_____

Classroom/School Box #_____

Box Inventory: Classroom/School

Classroom/School Box Label Color: ◯

Classroom/School Box #_____

Classroom/School Box #_____

Classroom/School Box #_____

Classroom/School Box #_____

Classroom/School Box #_____

Classroom/School Box #_____

Classroom/School Box #_____

Classroom/School Box #_____

Box Inventory: Theater Room

Theater Room Box Label Color:

Theater Room Box #______

Theater Room Box #______

Theater Room Box #______

Theater Room Box #______

Theater Room Box #______

Theater Room Box #______

Theater Room Box #______

Theater Room Box #______

Box Inventory: Theater Room

Theater Room Box Label Color: ◯

Theater Room Box #_____

Theater Room Box #_____

Theater Room Box #_____

Theater Room Box #_____

Theater Room Box #_____

Theater Room Box #_____

Theater Room Box #_____

Theater Room Box #_____

Box Inventory: Craft Room

Craft Room Box Label Color:

Craft Room Box #_____

Craft Room Box #_____

Craft Room Box #_____

Craft Room Box #_____

Craft Room Box #_____

Craft Room Box #_____

Craft Room Box #_____

Craft Room Box #_____

Box Inventory: Craft Room

Craft Room Box Label Color:

Craft Room Box #_____

Craft Room Box #_____

Craft Room Box #_____

Craft Room Box #_____

Craft Room Box #_____

Craft Room Box #_____

Craft Room Box #_____

Craft Room Box #_____

Box Inventory: Storage Room

Storage Room Box Label Color:

Storage Room Box #_____

Storage Room Box #_____

Storage Room Box #_____

Storage Room Box #_____

Storage Room Box #_____

Storage Room Box #_____

Storage Room Box #_____

Storage Room Box #_____

Box Inventory: Storage Room

Storage Room Box Label Color:

Storage Room Box #______

Storage Room Box #______

Storage Room Box #______

Storage Room Box #______

Storage Room Box #______

Storage Room Box #______

Storage Room Box #______

Storage Room Box #______

Box Inventory: Attic

Attic Box Label Color:

Attic Box #_____

Attic Box #_____

Attic Box #_____

Attic Box #_____

Attic Box #_____

Attic Box #_____

Attic Box #_____

Attic Box #_____

Box Inventory: Attic

Attic Box Label Color:

Attic Box #_____

Attic Box #_____

Attic Box #_____

Attic Box #_____

Attic Box #_____

Attic Box #_____

Attic Box #_____

Attic Box #_____

Box Inventory: Basement

Basement Box Label Color:

Basement Box #_____

Basement Box #_____

Basement Box #_____

Basement Box #_____

Basement Box #_____

Basement Box #_____

Basement Box #_____

Basement Box #_____

Box Inventory: Basement

Basement Box Label Color: ◯

Basement Box #_____

Basement Box #_____

Basement Box #_____

Basement Box #_____

Basement Box #_____

Basement Box #_____

Basement Box #_____

Basement Box #_____

Box Inventory: Workshop

Workshop Box Label Color:

Workshop Box #_____

Workshop Box #_____

Workshop Box #_____

Workshop Box #_____

Workshop Box #_____

Workshop Box #_____

Workshop Box #_____

Workshop Box #_____

Box Inventory: Workshop

Workshop Box Label Color:

Workshop Box #______

Workshop Box #______

Workshop Box #______

Workshop Box #______

Workshop Box #______

Workshop Box #______

Workshop Box #______

Workshop Box #______

Box Inventory: Garage

Garage Box Label Color:

Garage Box #_____

Garage Box #_____

Garage Box #_____

Garage Box #_____

Garage Box #_____

Garage Box #_____

Garage Box #_____

Garage Box #_____

Box Inventory: Garage

Garage Box Label Color: ◯

Garage Box #_____

Garage Box #_____

Garage Box #_____

Garage Box #_____

Garage Box #_____

Garage Box #_____

Garage Box #_____

Garage Box #_____

Box Inventory: Shed

Shed Box Label Color:

Shed Box #______

Shed Box #______

Shed Box #______

Shed Box #______

Shed Box #______

Shed Box #______

Shed Box #______

Shed Box #______

Box Inventory: Shed

Shed Box Label Color:

Shed Box #______

Shed Box #______

Shed Box #______

Shed Box #______

Shed Box #______

Shed Box #______

Shed Box #______

Shed Box #______

Box Inventory: Donate

Donate Box Label Color:

Donate Box #_____

Donate Box #_____

Donate Box #_____

Donate Box #_____

Donate Box #_____

Donate Box #_____

Donate Box #_____

Donate Box #_____

Box Inventory: Donate

Donate Box Label Color:

Donate Box #_____

Donate Box #_____

Donate Box #_____

Donate Box #_____

Donate Box #_____

Donate Box #_____

Donate Box #_____

Donate Box #_____

Box Inventory:

_____________ Box Label Color:

Box #______

Box #______

Box #______

Box #______

Box #______

Box #______

Box #______

Box #______

Box Inventory:

____________ Box Label Color: ◯

Box #_____

Box #_____

Box #_____

Box #_____

Box #_____

Box #_____

Box #_____

Box #_____

Box Inventory:

______________ Box Label Color:

Box #______

Box #______

Box #______

Box #______

Box #______

Box #______

Box #______

Box #______

Box Inventory:

_____________ Box Label Color:

Box #_____

Box #_____

Box #_____

Box #_____

Box #_____

Box #_____

Box #_____

Box #_____

MOVING DAY TIMELINE

Don't Forget!	Supplies	Meals & Snacks

Time: Name: Goal/Activity:	Time: Name: Goal/Activity:
Time: Name: Goal/Activity:	Time: Name: Goal/Activity:
Time: Name: Goal/Activity:	Time: Name: Goal/Activity:
Time: Name: Goal/Activity:	Time: Name: Goal/Activity:
Time: Name: Goal/Activity:	Time: Name: Goal/Activity:

MOVING DAY HELPERS:

Name: Ph #: Arrival Time: # Hours: Payment	Name: Ph #: Arrival Time: # Hours: Payment
Name: Ph #: Arrival Time: # Hours: Payment	Name: Ph #: Arrival Time: # Hours: Payment

Truck Rental:

Moving Company:

MOVING DAY: MOVERS, HELPERS, CLEANING & PACKING

Moving Company Name: Ph #: Truck Size: Estimated # Boxes: Estimated # Hours — Actual # Hours: Estimated Cost: — Actual Cost: Payment: Tip: Additional Equipment: Scheduled Arrival Time: — Actual Arrival : Start Time: — Completion Time Names of Movers:	Notes:

Truck Rental Location:

Ph #:
Truck Size:
Pick Up Date & Time:
Promised Return Date & Time:
Return Location:
Truck Cost:
Mileage:
Gas:
Additional Equipment:

Name: Ph #: Arrival Time: # Hours: Payment	Name: Ph #: Arrival Time: # Hours: Payment
Name: Ph #: Arrival Time: # Hours: Payment	Name: Ph #: Arrival Time: # Hours: Payment

Packing Company: Unpacking Company:	Old Home Cleaning Service:: New Home Cleaning Service:

NEW HOUSE: FURNITURE ARRIVAL CHECK LIST

Furniture for Room:			Notes
❑ ______	❑ ______	❑ ______	
❑ ______	❑ ______	❑ ______	
❑ ______	❑ ______	❑ ______	
❑ ______	❑ ______	❑ ______	

Furniture for Room:			Notes
❑ ______	❑ ______	❑ ______	
❑ ______	❑ ______	❑ ______	
❑ ______	❑ ______	❑ ______	
❑ ______	❑ ______	❑ ______	

Furniture for Room:			Notes
❑ ______	❑ ______	❑ ______	
❑ ______	❑ ______	❑ ______	
❑ ______	❑ ______	❑ ______	
❑ ______	❑ ______	❑ ______	

Furniture for Room:			Notes
❑ ______	❑ ______	❑ ______	
❑ ______	❑ ______	❑ ______	
❑ ______	❑ ______	❑ ______	
❑ ______	❑ ______	❑ ______	

Furniture for Room:			Notes
❑ ______	❑ ______	❑ ______	
❑ ______	❑ ______	❑ ______	
❑ ______	❑ ______	❑ ______	
❑ ______	❑ ______	❑ ______	

Furniture for Room:			Notes
❑ ______	❑ ______	❑ ______	
❑ ______	❑ ______	❑ ______	
❑ ______	❑ ______	❑ ______	
❑ ______	❑ ______	❑ ______	

Additional Items

©2024 Wildrose Media www.wildrose-media.com

NEW HOUSE: FURNITURE ARRIVAL CHECK LIST

Furniture for Room:			Notes
☐ ____________	☐ ____________	☐ ____________	
☐ ____________	☐ ____________	☐ ____________	
☐ ____________	☐ ____________	☐ ____________	
☐ ____________	☐ ____________	☐ ____________	

Furniture for Room:			Notes
☐ ____________	☐ ____________	☐ ____________	
☐ ____________	☐ ____________	☐ ____________	
☐ ____________	☐ ____________	☐ ____________	
☐ ____________	☐ ____________	☐ ____________	

Furniture for Room:			Notes
☐ ____________	☐ ____________	☐ ____________	
☐ ____________	☐ ____________	☐ ____________	
☐ ____________	☐ ____________	☐ ____________	
☐ ____________	☐ ____________	☐ ____________	

Furniture for Room:			Notes
☐ ____________	☐ ____________	☐ ____________	
☐ ____________	☐ ____________	☐ ____________	
☐ ____________	☐ ____________	☐ ____________	
☐ ____________	☐ ____________	☐ ____________	

Furniture for Room:			Notes
☐ ____________	☐ ____________	☐ ____________	
☐ ____________	☐ ____________	☐ ____________	
☐ ____________	☐ ____________	☐ ____________	
☐ ____________	☐ ____________	☐ ____________	

Furniture for Room:			Notes
☐ ____________	☐ ____________	☐ ____________	
☐ ____________	☐ ____________	☐ ____________	
☐ ____________	☐ ____________	☐ ____________	
☐ ____________	☐ ____________	☐ ____________	

Additional Items

NEW HOUSE: BOX ARRIVAL CHECK LIST

Boxes for Room:	Box Color Code: ⬭	Notes
☐ #1 ☐ ___		

Boxes for Room:	Box Color Code: ⬭	Notes
☐ ___ ☐ ___		

Boxes for Room:	Box Color Code: ⬭	Notes
☐ ___ ☐ ___		

Boxes for Room:	Box Color Code: ⬭	Notes
☐ ___ ☐ ___		

Boxes for Room:	Box Color Code: ⬭	Notes
☐ ___ ☐ ___		

Boxes for Room:	Box Color Code: ⬭	Notes
☐ ___ ☐ ___		

Additional Items

©2024 Wildrose Media www.wildrose-media.com

NEW HOUSE: BOX ARRIVAL CHECK LIST

Boxes for Room:				Box Color Code:		Notes
☐ #1	☐ ___	☐ ___	☐ ___	☐ ___	☐ ___	
☐ ___	☐ ___	☐ ___	☐ ___	☐ ___	☐ ___	
☐ ___	☐ ___	☐ ___	☐ ___	☐ ___	☐ ___	
☐ ___	☐ ___	☐ ___	☐ ___	☐ ___	☐ ___	

Boxes for Room:				Box Color Code:		Notes
☐ ___	☐ ___	☐ ___	☐ ___	☐ ___	☐ ___	
☐ ___	☐ ___	☐ ___	☐ ___	☐ ___	☐ ___	
☐ ___	☐ ___	☐ ___	☐ ___	☐ ___	☐ ___	
☐ ___	☐ ___	☐ ___	☐ ___	☐ ___	☐ ___	

Boxes for Room:				Box Color Code:		Notes
☐ ___	☐ ___	☐ ___	☐ ___	☐ ___	☐ ___	
☐ ___	☐ ___	☐ ___	☐ ___	☐ ___	☐ ___	
☐ ___	☐ ___	☐ ___	☐ ___	☐ ___	☐ ___	
☐ ___	☐ ___	☐ ___	☐ ___	☐ ___	☐ ___	

Boxes for Room:				Box Color Code:		Notes
☐ ___	☐ ___	☐ ___	☐ ___	☐ ___	☐ ___	
☐ ___	☐ ___	☐ ___	☐ ___	☐ ___	☐ ___	
☐ ___	☐ ___	☐ ___	☐ ___	☐ ___	☐ ___	
☐ ___	☐ ___	☐ ___	☐ ___	☐ ___	☐ ___	

Boxes for Room:				Box Color Code:		Notes
☐ ___	☐ ___	☐ ___	☐ ___	☐ ___	☐ ___	
☐ ___	☐ ___	☐ ___	☐ ___	☐ ___	☐ ___	
☐ ___	☐ ___	☐ ___	☐ ___	☐ ___	☐ ___	
☐ ___	☐ ___	☐ ___	☐ ___	☐ ___	☐ ___	

Boxes for Room:				Box Color Code:		Notes
☐ ___	☐ ___	☐ ___	☐ ___	☐ ___	☐ ___	
☐ ___	☐ ___	☐ ___	☐ ___	☐ ___	☐ ___	
☐ ___	☐ ___	☐ ___	☐ ___	☐ ___	☐ ___	
☐ ___	☐ ___	☐ ___	☐ ___	☐ ___	☐ ___	

Additional Items

©2024 Wildrose Media www.wildrose-media.com

NEW HOUSE: BOX ARRIVAL CHECK LIST

Boxes for Room: Box Color Code: ⬭   Notes

☐ #1 ☐ ___ ☐ ___ ☐ ___ ☐ ___ ☐ ___
☐ ___ ☐ ___ ☐ ___ ☐ ___ ☐ ___ ☐ ___
☐ ___ ☐ ___ ☐ ___ ☐ ___ ☐ ___ ☐ ___
☐ ___ ☐ ___ ☐ ___ ☐ ___ ☐ ___ ☐ ___

Boxes for Room: Box Color Code: ⬭   Notes

☐ ___ ☐ ___ ☐ ___ ☐ ___ ☐ ___ ☐ ___
☐ ___ ☐ ___ ☐ ___ ☐ ___ ☐ ___ ☐ ___
☐ ___ ☐ ___ ☐ ___ ☐ ___ ☐ ___ ☐ ___
☐ ___ ☐ ___ ☐ ___ ☐ ___ ☐ ___ ☐ ___

Boxes for Room: Box Color Code: ⬭   Notes

☐ ___ ☐ ___ ☐ ___ ☐ ___ ☐ ___ ☐ ___
☐ ___ ☐ ___ ☐ ___ ☐ ___ ☐ ___ ☐ ___
☐ ___ ☐ ___ ☐ ___ ☐ ___ ☐ ___ ☐ ___
☐ ___ ☐ ___ ☐ ___ ☐ ___ ☐ ___ ☐ ___

Boxes for Room: Box Color Code: ⬭   Notes

☐ ___ ☐ ___ ☐ ___ ☐ ___ ☐ ___ ☐ ___
☐ ___ ☐ ___ ☐ ___ ☐ ___ ☐ ___ ☐ ___
☐ ___ ☐ ___ ☐ ___ ☐ ___ ☐ ___ ☐ ___
☐ ___ ☐ ___ ☐ ___ ☐ ___ ☐ ___ ☐ ___

Boxes for Room: Box Color Code: ⬭   Notes

☐ ___ ☐ ___ ☐ ___ ☐ ___ ☐ ___ ☐ ___
☐ ___ ☐ ___ ☐ ___ ☐ ___ ☐ ___ ☐ ___
☐ ___ ☐ ___ ☐ ___ ☐ ___ ☐ ___ ☐ ___
☐ ___ ☐ ___ ☐ ___ ☐ ___ ☐ ___ ☐ ___

Boxes for Room: Box Color Code: ⬭   Notes

☐ ___ ☐ ___ ☐ ___ ☐ ___ ☐ ___ ☐ ___
☐ ___ ☐ ___ ☐ ___ ☐ ___ ☐ ___ ☐ ___
☐ ___ ☐ ___ ☐ ___ ☐ ___ ☐ ___ ☐ ___
☐ ___ ☐ ___ ☐ ___ ☐ ___ ☐ ___ ☐ ___

Additional Items

©2024 Wildrose Media www.wildrose-media.com

NEW HOUSE: BOX ARRIVAL CHECK LIST

Boxes for Room: Box Color Code: ⬭ | Notes

☐ #1	☐ ___	☐ ___	☐ ___	☐ ___	☐ ___
☐ ___	☐ ___	☐ ___	☐ ___	☐ ___	☐ ___
☐ ___	☐ ___	☐ ___	☐ ___	☐ ___	☐ ___
☐ ___	☐ ___	☐ ___	☐ ___	☐ ___	☐ ___

Boxes for Room: Box Color Code: ⬭ | Notes

☐ ___	☐ ___	☐ ___	☐ ___	☐ ___	☐ ___
☐ ___	☐ ___	☐ ___	☐ ___	☐ ___	☐ ___
☐ ___	☐ ___	☐ ___	☐ ___	☐ ___	☐ ___
☐ ___	☐ ___	☐ ___	☐ ___	☐ ___	☐ ___

Boxes for Room: Box Color Code: ⬭ | Notes

☐ ___	☐ ___	☐ ___	☐ ___	☐ ___	☐ ___
☐ ___	☐ ___	☐ ___	☐ ___	☐ ___	☐ ___
☐ ___	☐ ___	☐ ___	☐ ___	☐ ___	☐ ___
☐ ___	☐ ___	☐ ___	☐ ___	☐ ___	☐ ___

Boxes for Room: Box Color Code: ⬭ | Notes

☐ ___	☐ ___	☐ ___	☐ ___	☐ ___	☐ ___
☐ ___	☐ ___	☐ ___	☐ ___	☐ ___	☐ ___
☐ ___	☐ ___	☐ ___	☐ ___	☐ ___	☐ ___
☐ ___	☐ ___	☐ ___	☐ ___	☐ ___	☐ ___

Boxes for Room: Box Color Code: ⬭ | Notes

☐ ___	☐ ___	☐ ___	☐ ___	☐ ___	☐ ___
☐ ___	☐ ___	☐ ___	☐ ___	☐ ___	☐ ___
☐ ___	☐ ___	☐ ___	☐ ___	☐ ___	☐ ___
☐ ___	☐ ___	☐ ___	☐ ___	☐ ___	☐ ___

Boxes for Room: Box Color Code: ⬭ | Notes

☐ ___	☐ ___	☐ ___	☐ ___	☐ ___	☐ ___
☐ ___	☐ ___	☐ ___	☐ ___	☐ ___	☐ ___
☐ ___	☐ ___	☐ ___	☐ ___	☐ ___	☐ ___
☐ ___	☐ ___	☐ ___	☐ ___	☐ ___	☐ ___

Additional Items

©2024 Wildrose Media www.wildrose-media.com

CLEANING CHECKLIST

.Front Entrance
- ❑ Light Fixture
- ❑ Walls
- ❑ Windows
- ❑ Wall Plates
- ❑ Baseboards
- ❑ Vacuum Floor
- ❑ Wash Floor

Living Room
- ❑ Ceiling Fan
- ❑ Light Fixture
- ❑ Walls
- ❑ Windows
- ❑ Wall Plates
- ❑ Baseboards
- ❑ Vacuum Floor
- ❑ Wash Floor
- ❑ Steam Clean Carpet
- ❑ Doors

Dining Room
- ❑ Ceiling Fan
- ❑ Light Fixture
- ❑ Walls
- ❑ Windows
- ❑ Wall Plates
- ❑ Baseboards
- ❑ Vacuum Floor
- ❑ Wash Floor
- ❑ Steam Clean Carpet
- ❑ Doors

Laundry Area
- ❑ Light Fixture
- ❑ Walls
- ❑ Windows
- ❑ Wall Plates
- ❑ Baseboards
- ❑ Vacuum Floor
- ❑ Wash Floor
- ❑ Dryer Vents

Family Room
- ❑ Ceiling Fan
- ❑ Light Fixture
- ❑ Walls
- ❑ Windows
- ❑ Wall Plates
- ❑ Baseboards
- ❑ Vacuum Floor
- ❑ Wash Floor
- ❑ Steam Clean Carpet
- ❑ Doors

Office/Den
- ❑ Ceiling Fan
- ❑ Light Fixture
- ❑ Walls
- ❑ Windows
- ❑ Wall Plates
- ❑ Baseboards
- ❑ Empty & Wipe Shelves
- ❑ Vacuum Floor
- ❑ Wash Floor
- ❑ Steam Clean Carpet
- ❑ Doors

Kitchen
- ❑ Empty/Wipe Fridge
- ❑ Empty/Wipe Freezer
- ❑ Clean Microwave
- ❑ Clean Oven
- ❑ Clean Stovetop/Burners
- ❑ Clean Exhaust Fan/Hood
- ❑ Empty & Wipe Out Cabinets
- ❑ Wipe Cabinet Door Knobs
- ❑ Clean Countertop/Back Splash
- ❑ Empty Dishwasher
- ❑ Clean Kitchen Sink
- ❑ Unplug Appliances
- ❑ Ceiling Fan
- ❑ Light Fixture
- ❑ Walls
- ❑ Windows
- ❑ Wall Plates
- ❑ Baseboards
- ❑ Vacuum Floor
- ❑ Wash Floor
- ❑ Wipe Doors/Door Knobs

Pantry
- ❑ Empty Shelves
- ❑ Wipe Shelves
- ❑ Light Fixture
- ❑ Walls
- ❑ Windows
- ❑ Wall Plates
- ❑ Baseboards
- ❑ Vacuum Floor
- ❑ Wash Floor
- ❑ Wipe Door Knobs/Handles

Closets
- ❑ Front Closet
- ❑ Hall Closet
- ❑ Linen Closet
- ❑ ________________
- ❑ ________________
- ❑ ________________

Other
- ❑ Fireplace #1
- ❑ Fireplace #2
- ❑ Wood-burning/Pellet Stove
- ❑ Septic Pumped
- ❑ Front Porch
- ❑ Sunroom
- ❑ Back Porch/Deck
- ❑ Patio
- ❑ Attic
- ❑ Basement
- ❑ Shed
- ❑ Workshop
- ❑ Garage/Carport
- ❑ ________________
- ❑ ________________

Bedrooms	Mstr Bdrm	Bdrm 1	Bdrm 2	Bdrm 3	Bdrm 4	
Ceiling Fan						
Light Fixture						
Walls						
Windows						
Wall Plates						
Baseboards						
Closet						
Vacuum Floor						
Wash Floor						
Steam Clean Carpet						
Doors & Knobs						

Bathrooms	Mstr B	Bath 1	Bath 2	Bath 3
Vent Fan				
Sinks/Countertop				
Cabinet				
Medicine Cabinet				
Tub/Shower				
Light Fixture				
Walls/Baseboards				
Windows				
Vacuum/Wash Floor				
Doors & Knobs				

©2024 Wildrose Media www.wildrose-media.com

UTILITIES DIRECTORY

Old Address Utilities						
Type	Acct #	Billing Date	Amount Due	Paid	Transfer/Shut Off Date	Notes
Gas						
Electric						
Internet						
Cable						
Water						
Sewer						
Trash						
Recycling						

New Address Utilities						
Type	Acct #	Billing Date	Amount Due	Paid	Transfer/Shut Off Date	Notes
Gas						
Electric						
Internet						
Cable						
Water						
Sewer						
Trash						
Recycling						

CHANGE OF ADDRESS

- ❑ Employer
- ❑ Employer
- ❑ Employer

- ❑ Utilities – Gas & Oil
- ❑ Utilities - Electricity
- ❑ Water
- ❑ Sewer
- ❑ Trash Collection
- ❑ Recycling Service
- ❑ Home Phone
- ❑ Mobile Phone Provider
- ❑ Mobile Phone Provider
- ❑ Cable
- ❑ Internet
- ❑ Online Services
    - ❑ Netflix
    - ❑ YouTube
    - ❑ Amazon
    - ❑ Other:
    - ❑ Other:
    - ❑ Other:

- ❑ Grocery Delivery Services
- ❑ Meal Delivery Services
- ❑ Lawn Care
- ❑ Pool Maintenance
- ❑ Cleaning Service
- ❑ Mechanic
- ❑ Handyman

- ❑ Veterinarian
- ❑ Pet Day Care
- ❑ Pet Groomer

- ❑ Religious Institution
- ❑ Volunteer Organization:
- ❑ Volunteer Organization:
- ❑ Public Library
- ❑ Gym Membership
- ❑ Club Memberships – AAA, Costco, Sam's, etc.
- ❑ AARP
- ❑ Magazine Subscriptions
- ❑ Newspaper Subscriptions

- ❑ USPS Mail Forwarding
- ❑ Immigration/Green Card/Passport Services
- ❑ DMV - Vehicle Registration
- ❑ MVA - Drivers License
- ❑ Social Security Administration
- ❑ WIC, SNAP

- ❑ Family & Friends

- ❑ School:
- ❑ School:
- ❑ School:
- ❑ Daycare
- ❑ Nanny
- ❑ Babysitter

- ❑ Lawyer
- ❑ Accountant
- ❑ Tax Preparation
- ❑ Internal Revenue Service
- ❑ Voter Registration
- ❑ Investment Services
- ❑ Financial Planner
- ❑ Bank:
- ❑ Bank:
- ❑ Bank:
- ❑ Credit Card Companies
- ❑ Student Loans
- ❑ Vehicle Loans
- ❑ Personal Loans

- ❑ Homeowners Insurance
- ❑ Vehicle Insurance
- ❑ Life Insurance
- ❑ Health Insurance
- ❑ Prescription Insurance
- ❑ Short term/Long-term Care Insurance
- ❑ Dental Insurance

- ❑ Primary Care Physician
- ❑ Pediatrician
- ❑ Specialist:
- ❑ Specialist:
- ❑ Specialist:
- ❑ Specialist:
- ❑ Optometrist
- ❑ Eye Wear Provider
- ❑ Audiologist
- ❑ Chiropractor
- ❑ Psychologist/Psychiatrist
- ❑ General Dentist
- ❑ Pediatric Dentist
- ❑ Orthodontist/Endodontist
- ❑ Pharmacy #1
- ❑ Pharmacy #2
- ❑ Update 911 Location
- ❑ Physical Therapy
- ❑ Acupuncturist
- ❑ Chiropractor
- ❑ Rehab Facility
- ❑ Adult Daycare Facility
- ❑ Disability Transportation Services

©2024 Wildrose Media www.wildrose-media.com

Wildrose Media website
Home Page

Faith Family Fun Blog

Wildrose Media website
Shop Page

Additional books from Wildrose Media, available on Amazon:

Sermon Notebook
Kids Ages 9-12 years
Cross cover

Sermon Notebook
Kids Ages 6-8 years
Bunny cover

The Birth of Jesus
Coloring Book

The Story of Easter
Coloring Book
Blue cover

Bible Teaching
Sheets
Old Testament - KJV

Bible Teaching Sheets
New Testament - KJV

Friendship and Freedom
Story of the Statue of Liberty

100 Questions to Ask Myself
Vol.1 - pink cover

Ultimate Fishing Journal
for Kids Vol. 1

Ultimate Fishing Journal
for Girls - pink cover

Headache Diary, 5"x 6"
Symptom Notebook

Dutch Boy & Girl
Small Notebook 5"x6"

The above book QR codes are Amazon Affiliate links,
I may receive compensation from purchases made using these links,
at no additional cost to you.

Wildrose Media

www.wildrose-media.com

Made in the USA
Monee, IL
04 November 2026

67379476R00058